Brian Cox

Scientific Superstar!

First published in 2014 by Wayland

Copyright © Wayland 2014

Wayland
338 Euston Road
London
NW1 3BH

Wayland Australia
Level 17/207 Kent Street
Sydney NSW 2000

Senior editor: Julia Adams

Produced for Wayland by Dynamo
Written by Hettie Bingham

Picture acknowledgements:

Key: b=bottom, t=top, r=right, l=left,
m=middle, bgd=background

Alamy P2 tr, p11 br, p15 tr JEP Celebrity Photos; Getty Images
P1 m, p4 m, p5 tr, p9 b, p13 m, p17 mr, p19 tl, p20 b, p22 m, p24 mr,
p27 m, p29 br Getty Images; p16 br Gamma Rapho; Shutterstock
Backgrounds and Doodles: Martina Vaculikova, ILeysen, P.Jirawat,
PinkPueblo, Tsaplia, Marie Nimrichterova, Cologne82, dalmingo,
Lorelyn Medina, vector-RGB, blablalena, p5 mr fongfong, p6/7 m jorgen
mcleman, p14 ml iurii, p18 tl Dan Breckwoldt, p21 tr Dan Howell.

Dewey classification: 530'.092-dc23

ISBN 978 0 7502 8263 5
E-book ISBN 987 0 7502 8778 4

Printed in China
10 9 8 7 6 5 4 3 2 1

Wayland is a division of Hachette Children's Books,
an Hachette UK company.
www.hachette.co.uk

Brian Cox

Contents

BRIAN COX
The Poppy Professor!

■ Physicist, television presenter, astronomer, journalist and musician: Professor Brian Cox OBE is a man of many talents. His fascination with physics and the cosmos is infectious; he has inspired many young people across the world, ensuring that science plays a big part in popular culture today.

'SCIENCE IS TOO IMPORTANT NOT TO BE A PART OF POPULAR CULTURE.'

'EVERYONE'S INTERESTED IN SCIENCE IN SOME WAY, WHETHER IT'S LOOKING AT THE STARS OR ASKING WHY A LEAF IS GREEN... IT'S ABOUT DISCOVERING WHAT SCIENCE MEANS TO YOU.'

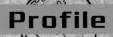

NAME: Brian Edward Cox

HONOURS: OBE

BORN: 3 March 1968

HEIGHT: 1.78 metres (5ft 10 inches)

FAMILY: Married to Gia Milinovich with stepson Moki and son George Eagle

HOMETOWN: Chadderton, Lancashire, England

SCHOOLS: Hulme Grammar School

UNIVERSITY: University of Manchester

OCCUPATION: Physicist, television presenter, broadcaster, journalist and former musician

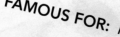

FAMOUS FOR: Presenting Wonders of Life, Wonders of the Universe, Wonders of the Solar System, working on the ATLAS experiment and playing keyboard in the band D:Ream

LIKES: Space, science, Oldham Athletic football club and music

CHILDHOOD

Head in the stars

From early on in his childhood, Brian has been fascinated by rockets, spacemen and the unanswered questions of the universe. He was just a toddler when he watched the Apollo 11 mission landing men on the moon. Later, with his treasured telescope, Brian studied the stars and dreamed of flying to Mars one day.

Brian was born on 3 March 1968 at the Oldham & District General Hospital. His mother, Barbara, and father, David, worked for banks; his mother as a cashier and his father a branch manager. Together with Brian's sister, Sandra, the family lived in Chadderton, Lancashire.

Big Bang!

of himself as one of 'Apollo's children' – of kids inspired by the Apollo 11 moon who grew up to become scientists and He hopes that the Large Hadron Collider where he works on a particle detector ATLAS, will have the same effect on ren growing up today (see page 16).

Born one year before the moon landings, Brian grew up with a sense of excitement about the space programme. His dad has told him that he watched the moon landings on television at the age of one, although he can't remember that far back. He does, however, remember seeing pictures of Apollo around the house. Brian had a sense that 'the early 1970s was a time of astonishing science' and a feeling that 'anything was possible'.

'I WAS ALWAYS FASCINATED BY THE NIGHT SKY; I GOT MY FIRST TELESCOPE WHEN I WAS SEVEN AND WAS CAPTIVATED.' I WAS A VERY, VERY, VERY NERDY CHILD.'

When Brian was six he began to collect astronomy cards, and at seven he got his first telescope for Christmas. For his tenth birthday he asked for a fuse box! He used this to wire his granddad's shed and light it up.

Brian would have liked to watch real rockets taking off and landing, but aircraft were the nearest thing he could find; every Sunday he would go plane spotting at Manchester Airport. 'I didn't go out of the country until I was 17, so it was a really romantic thing to see all these planes flying in from all over the world,' he once said.

Brian at School

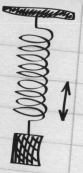

Brian's first school was Chadderton Hall, a primary school right next door to where he lived. He could even climb the fence to get home (when no one was looking). His head teacher was called Mr Perfect, and it seems that Brian thought the name was well-suited:

Brian's grandparents worked in the Manchester cotton mills and did not get any qualifications. They helped pay for Brian and his sister to be privately educated, in order to make sure that Brian and Sandra had the advantages which they had missed from their own early lives.

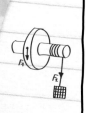

'(MR PERFECT) WAS BRILLIANT; HE RAN AFTER-SCHOOL CLASSES IN MATHS AND ENGLISH AND LET KIDS STAY ON TO PLAY BOARD GAMES. WHEN WE PLAYED RISK, WE WOULD DISCUSS EACH MOVE AND ONLY MAKE ONE OR TWO MOVES A WEEK, SO ONE GAME WOULD GO ON ALL TERM.'

When he was 11, Brian moved on to Hulme Grammar School, which was a private school. Having been disappointed that physics wasn't taught at primary school, this was a subject that he was especially keen to pursue at secondary school. His physics teacher, Mr Galloway, was a firm favourite with Brian.

'I WAS NEVER TOP OF THE CLASS; I WAS AROUND THE TOP. I THINK THE IDEA YOU HAVE TO BE A GENIUS TO BE A PROFESSIONAL SCIENTIST IS DESTRUCTIVE. WE NEED MORE CHILDREN TO BECOME SCIENTISTS.'

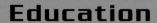

When Brian and his friends became interested in the synthesized music of the 1980s, it was Mr Galloway who helped them create the electronics they needed to make a 'noise gate'. This was a device that would work with the hi-hat cymbals on a drum kit to trigger syncopated chords on a keyboard.

Brian sat four A levels: physics, chemistry, general studies and maths. He did very well in everything apart from maths – he got a D grade. It was not until later in life that Brian realized he could do maths after all.

'I DIDN'T LIKE MATHS AT ALL IN SCHOOL, BUT I DID IT BECAUSE I LIKED PHYSICS AND I THOUGHT I HAD TO DO IT.'

Later in life, he began to see maths as more of a craft and something you have to work at and practise for hours, just like a musical instrument.

'I WAS ONE OF THOSE KIDS WHO'D BE VERY UPSET IF I GOT A DETENTION. I DIDN'T WANT TO DISAPPOINT.'

Living the
D:REAM!

Brian's interest in music continued to grow and he taught himself to play keyboard. It was when he went to a Duran Duran concert that Brian began to see music as a career option – he wanted to be a rock star!

It didn't take long for Brian to achieve his goal; he joined the rock group Dare in the 1980s as keyboard player and stayed with the band until 1991. He recorded two albums, *Out of the Silence* and *Blood from Stone*, both released by A&M records.

Big Bang!

Brian joined D:Ream by accident. He was only supposed to be filling in for someone, but ended up staying for years.

When Brian left Dare at the age of 23, he decided to return to his studies and began a degree in physics at Manchester University. But although he enjoyed his course, that wasn't to be the end of his music career.

In 1993, Brian joined the pop group D:Ream and found himself mixing his studies with appearances on *Top of the Pops*. 'Once I was in the lab all day and when I finished I walked up the road to support Take That at the G-Mex in Manchester. My friends at university just thought it was so funny,' Brian once said.

D:Ream's dance hit *Things Can Only Get Better* reached number one in the charts in 1994. The hit song resurfaced when it was used as the anthem for New Labour's election campaign in 1997.

There came a point when Brian had to decide whether to complete his physics degree or continue his life as a pop star. He decided to leave D:Ream and finish his degree. He gained a first class honours degree and stayed on at Manchester to complete a PhD. It was here that Brian attended lectures given by Jeff Forshaw, a professor of particle physics, who became a firm friend.

'PHYSICS EXCITED ME MORE [THAN MUSIC]. I FELT SO ENERGIZED BY THE PROCESS OF LEARNING – THE INTENSITY OF LEARNING – YOU DON'T GET THAT VERY OFTEN.'

Putting the *fizz* into
PHYSICS

From wiring his granddad's garden shed as a boy to becoming a professor at Manchester University, Brian has had a life-long relationship with physics.

Getting to the bottom of what makes the natural world around us work, is something that has interested Brian since he was a small boy. Physics is the study of matter (particles) and the way it moves through space and time. The study of physics helps us to understand the natural world and how the universe behaves, so helping us to develop new technologies. Without the study of physics we wouldn't have electricity, radio, television or computers.

Along with his other commitments, Brian teaches first-year students during the autumn term at Manchester University where he is a Particle Physics and Astronomy Research Council (PPARC) Advanced Fellow. He is course leader for the study of quantum physics and relativity. 'There's a moment when you walk into the lecture theatre and it's "Oh, there's that bloke on telly." But they forget within a minute because they've got to do an exam,' explained Brian.

Big Bang!

The word 'physics' is from the Greek word 'phusika' meaning natural things.

'MAYBE WE DON'T NOTICE IT BUT WE'RE IN A WORLD-LEADING POSITION, WITH A SCIENCE AND ENGINEERING BASE THAT'S BEEN BUILT UP OVER 400 YEARS. AND I HONESTLY BELIEVE THAT... SCIENCE AND TECHNOLOGY COULD TRANSFORM OUR ECONOMY.'

'WHAT SCIENTISTS ARE ATTACHED TO IS JOURNEYS INTO THE UNKNOWN AND DISCOVERING THINGS THAT ARE COMPLETELY UNEXPECTED AND BAFFLING AND SURPRISING.'

'THE IDEA THAT THERE'S NOTHING LEFT TO DISCOVER IS NONSENSE.'

'[SCIENCE] IS THE BASIS OF OUR CIVILIZATION; WE'D BE IN TREES IF SOMEBODY HADN'T TRIED TO WORK OUT HOW NATURE WORKS.'

Physics has become a much more popular subject to study over the past few years; it is thought that the popularity of Brian's television shows may have influenced this. The number of students taking degrees in physics went up by 50 per cent in the years between 2003 and 2011. Being a science geek is cool!

Starry-Eyed Brian

Brian has been obsessed with space for as long as he can remember; first with the Apollo moon landings and then with films such as *Star Wars* and *Star Trek*.

As he grew up Brian wanted to discover more about the universe, our solar system and the world we live in. He describes our civilization as a 'tiny flickering flame' in a vast universe. He points out that humans have existed for only 200,000 years which, in a universe that is thought to be 13.7 billion years old, is nothing more than a snapshot.

By continuing to explore the cosmos, Brian believes we can better understand our place in this universe. Ours is the only planet known to have life, but Brian believes that there is still a lot left to be discovered. Here are some of the ideas that fascinate Brian:

IN OUR 200,000 YEARS ON THIS PLANET WE'VE MADE REMARKABLE PROGRESS. IT WAS ONLY 2,500 YEARS AGO THAT WE BELIEVED THAT THE SUN WAS A GOD AND WE MEASURED ITS ORBIT WITH STONE TOWERS BUILT ON THE TOP OF A HILL. TODAY... WE HAVE OBSERVATORIES THAT ARE ALMOST INFINITELY MORE SOPHISTICATED THAN THOSE TOWERS SO THAT WE CAN GAZE DEEP INTO THE UNIVERSE.

(NOW) WE CAN SEE EXACTLY WHAT IT IS THAT WE DON'T UNDERSTAND. WE CAN SEE, FOR EXAMPLE, THAT THE UNIVERSE IS ACCELERATING IN ITS EXPANSION, IT'S JUST THAT WE DON'T UNDERSTAND WHY... YET.

WE LIVE ON A WORLD OF WONDERS; A PLACE OF ASTONISHING BEAUTY AND COMPLEXITY. WE HAVE VAST OCEANS AND INCREDIBLE WEATHER, GIANT MOUNTAINS AND BREATH-TAKING LANDSCAPES... WE'RE PART OF A MUCH WIDER ECOSYSTEM THAT EXTENDS WAY BEYOND THE TOP OF OUR ATMOSPHERE.

Brian and the ATLAS Experiment

Scientists at CERN have been working on experiments to learn more about the universe by making their own Big Bang! Brian has been working as part of a team there on the **ATLAS** experiment.

CERN stands for Centre Européen pour la recherche nucléaire, which is French and translates as European Centre for Nuclear Research. The Large Hadron Collider (LHC) is CERN's particle accelerator – a machine that makes particles move very fast. ATLAS is one of the experiments being carried out to learn about and follow high energy particles.

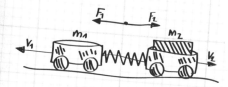

The ATLAS experiment uses special equipment called toroidal (ring-shaped) LHC apparatus. The scientists are using it to try to copy the Big Bang by sending particles in opposite directions around the ring at very high speed, so that they crash into each other. The scientists observe closely to try to learn more about the building blocks of the universe. Brian's job on the project is to analyse the data as it comes in.

Brian is one of thousands of scientists who have joined the experiments at CERN from over 100 countries around the world. These experiments led to the discovery of the Higgs particle (a particle that fills everything in the universe, including what we think of as empty space). Brian believes that is the most important discovery in his lifetime as it will help scientists to discover how we came to be here.

'THE AIM OF PARTICLE PHYSICS IS TO UNDERSTAND WHAT EVERYTHING'S MADE OF, AND HOW EVERYTHING STICKS TOGETHER. BY EVERYTHING I MEAN ME AND YOU, THE EARTH, THE SUN, THE 100 BILLION SUNS IN OUR GALAXY AND THE 100 BILLION GALAXIES IN THE OBSERVABLE UNIVERSE. ABSOLUTELY EVERYTHING.'

Big Bang!

Experiments at CERN can consume up to 180,000,000 watts of electricity. To give you something to compare this with, the average computer uses less than 250 watts.

The LHC doesn't need to be shaped in a ring; this was done simply to save space. Brian would have preferred it to be in a line – the longer the better!

Brian's Broadcasts

British Academy TV awards

Brian got into television almost by accident. He was being interviewed along with other scientists at CERN for the television documentary Horizon, and the producers spotted his potential.

Brian featured in various Horizon documentaries on BBC Two, first introducing his work at CERN and then as a presenter. The Horizon programmes he featured in were: Einstein's Equation of Life and Death (2005); Einstein's Unfinished Symphony (2005); The Six Billion Dollar Experiment (2007); What on Earth is Wrong with Gravity? (2008); Do You Know What Time It Is? (2008); Can We Make a Star on Earth? (2009).

Also for BBC Two, Brian presented the documentary series Wonders of the Solar System in 2010. This was a series of five episodes, each one featuring a different aspect of our solar system. It was an enormous success and Brian went on to present Wonders of the Universe in 2011 and Wonders of Life in 2013 – both extremely popular.

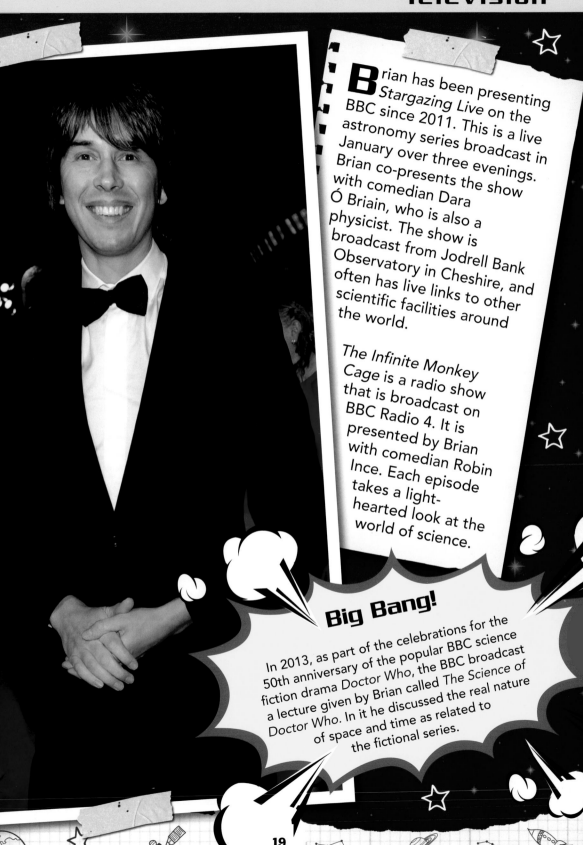

Brian has been presenting *Stargazing Live* on the BBC since 2011. This is a live astronomy series broadcast in January over three evenings. Brian co-presents the show with comedian Dara Ó Briain, who is also a physicist. The show is broadcast from Jodrell Bank Observatory in Cheshire, and often has live links to other scientific facilities around the world.

The Infinite Monkey Cage is a radio show that is broadcast on BBC Radio 4. It is presented by Brian with comedian Robin Ince. Each episode takes a light-hearted look at the world of science.

Big Bang!

In 2013, as part of the celebrations for the 50th anniversary of the popular BBC science fiction drama Doctor Who, the BBC broadcast a lecture given by Brian called *The Science of Doctor Who*. In it he discussed the real nature of space and time as related to the fictional series.

Awards and Honours

The way in which Brian explains physics to his audience is always interesting and fun. He has made the public more aware of physics and its importance in the modern world. It is for this that he has received many prestigious awards.

2006

IN 2006, BRIAN RECEIVED THE BRITISH ASSOCIATION'S LORD KELVIN AWARD FOR HIS WORK AS A FELLOW OF THE EXPLORERS CLUB. THIS IS A PROFESSIONAL SOCIETY BASED IN THE UNITED STATES OF AMERICA WHICH IS DEDICATED TO THE EXPLORATION OF THE EARTH, ITS OCEANS AND OUTER SPACE.

2010

IN 2010, BRIAN RECEIVED THE INSTITUTE OF PHYSICS KELVIN PRIZE. THIS IS AN AWARD ESTABLISHED BY THE INSTITUTE OF PHYSICS IN 1994, FOR PEOPLE WHO HAVE HELPED PROMOTE THE PUBLIC'S UNDERSTANDING OF PHYSICS.

IN THE QUEEN'S 2010 BIRTHDAY HONOURS, BRIAN WAS APPOINTED OFFICER OF THE ORDER OF THE BRITISH EMPIRE (OBE) FOR HIS SERVICES TO SCIENCE.

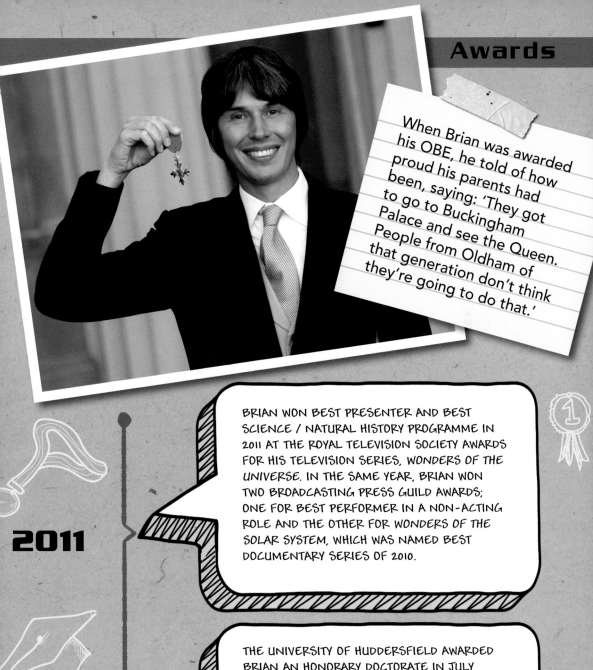

When Brian was awarded his OBE, he told of how proud his parents had been, saying: 'They got to go to Buckingham Palace and see the Queen. People from Oldham of that generation don't think they're going to do that.'

2011

BRIAN WON BEST PRESENTER AND BEST SCIENCE / NATURAL HISTORY PROGRAMME IN 2011 AT THE ROYAL TELEVISION SOCIETY AWARDS FOR HIS TELEVISION SERIES, WONDERS OF THE UNIVERSE. IN THE SAME YEAR, BRIAN WON TWO BROADCASTING PRESS GUILD AWARDS; ONE FOR BEST PERFORMER IN A NON-ACTING ROLE AND THE OTHER FOR WONDERS OF THE SOLAR SYSTEM, WHICH WAS NAMED BEST DOCUMENTARY SERIES OF 2010.

2012

THE UNIVERSITY OF HUDDERSFIELD AWARDED BRIAN AN HONORARY DOCTORATE IN JULY 2012. LATER THAT YEAR HE WAS AWARDED AN HONORARY DOCTORATE BY THE OPEN UNIVERSITY FOR HIS 'EXCEPTIONAL CONTRIBUTION TO EDUCATION AND CULTURE'. ALSO THAT YEAR, BRIAN WAS AWARDED THE INSTITUTE OF PHYSICS PRESIDENT'S MEDAL, WHICH WAS HANDED OVER BY THE ACTOR SIR PATRICK STEWART, FAMOUS FOR HIS ROLE IN THE TELEVISION SERIES STAR TREK: THE NEXT GENERATION.

Family Life

Brian is married to Gia Milinovich. They have a son, George Eagle, and Brian is step-dad to Gia's son, Moki, from her previous marriage.

Brian's wife, Gia, is from Minnesota in the United States of America but has lived in the United Kingdom for almost 20 years. She is a television presenter, writer and blogger. She is the new media adviser to media personality Jonathan Ross, and is responsible for setting up his Twitter account. She is an expert on computers, technology, the Internet and science. She has many interests, including British comedy, ancient Egypt and the Apollo moon landings.

Brian Cox and Gia Milinovich attend a screening of Gravity in November 2013.

Brian first met Gia in London when they were both working as panellists on a web seminar. Gia had been impressed that Brian worked at CERN. Their first date was in Manchester on 11 September 2001 – the day of the terrorist attack in New York on the World Trade Center. They spent their time glued to a news channel as they both had many friends in New York and were worried for their safety. 'It was a very bonding experience,' Brian said.

NEW YORK, SEPTEMBER 11
Clouds of smoke rise from fires at the World Trade Center Towers as a result of a terrorist attack.

Brian and Gia's son, George Eagle, was born in 2009. Eagle was the name given to the lunar module of Apollo 11, the first spacecraft to land humans on the moon. Brian and Gia both thought this was a fitting name for their son. The first piece of music that their newborn son ever heard was Saturn 5 by Inspiral Carpets. It was a song that reminded Brian of the moon landings. We thought, 'What would be appropriate for his entrance into the world?' said Brian.

Big Bang!

When Brian and Gia got married in 2003, they didn't tell anyone – not even their parents. 'We felt quite strongly that it was about us and not anybody else,' he later explained.

What Does Brian Believe?

Brian is an atheist, which means that he does not believe in a god. He has said that he would like society to move forward in a more rational way, but he is not anti-religion. He accepts that people have different ideas of how the universe came about. However, he does think that people should not take the Bible literally.

'I WAS SENT TO SUNDAY SCHOOL FOR A FEW WEEKS BUT I DIDN'T LIKE GETTING UP ON SUNDAY MORNINGS. BUT SOME OF MY FRIENDS ARE RELIGIOUS. I DON'T HAVE A STRONG VIEW ON RELIGION, OTHER THAN ILLOGICAL RELIGION.'

Brian believes that there is common ground between the scientific approach to the world and the religious approach. He thinks that in both cases people have noticed that there is something beautiful and worth understanding. 'That's much more important than not noticing,' says Brian.

'SCIENCE IS NOT ARROGANT; IT DOESN'T CONSIDER EVERYTHING IT DOES TO BE RIGHT. THERE WILL BE ANOTHER, BETTER THEORY OF GRAVITY IN THE FUTURE, FOR EXAMPLE. BUT IT IS VERY GOOD AT SHOWING WHEN THINGS ARE WRONG.'

Brian has said that there is 'a lot of goodwill towards scientists from the religious communities in this country'. He once met the Dean of Guildford Cathedral while taking part in a religious debate on television. Brian was there to give his opinion as an atheist. The Dean was very interested in Brian's work at CERN and so Brian took him there on a visit and they became good friends.

Once Brian was invited to Lambeth Palace by Rowan Williams, the 104th Archbishop of Canterbury, who had enjoyed Brian's series Wonders of the Solar System.

'AS FAR AS I'M CONCERNED WE'RE INFORMATION PROCESSING DEVICES, SO WE'RE PROCESSING INFORMATION... WHICH REQUIRES ENERGY... AND SO WE GENERATE THAT BY EATING FOOD AND CONVERTING IT INTO ENERGY... SO IF YOU STOP PROVIDING THE POWER SOURCE THEN YOU STOP PROCESSING INFORMATION.'

(BRIAN ON WHY HE DOESN'T BELIEVE IN AN AFTERLIFE)

Early Influences

The Apollo moon landings certainly inspired Brian's interest in space and physics, but who were the influences in Brian's life?

When Brian was just 12 years old, he watched a science documentary on television that changed his life. The programme was Carl Sagan's *Cosmos: A Personal Voyage*.

'It was the thing that really convinced me I should be a scientist,'

Brian said about it.

'I'd been interested in astronomy for many years, but just seeing that on television; Sagan's unique … approach to science just captured my imagination.'

Planetary scientist, Carl Sagan

Carl Sagan was a planetary scientist and astronomer born in Brooklyn, USA in 1934. Like Brian, he communicated his ideas to a popular audience and wrote many books on the subject. From an early age Carl Sagan had been interested in nature. He wanted to know what stars were and his parents weren't able to give him an answer. So he began to visit the library on his own from the age of five.

Carl Sagan later studied at the University of Chicago during the 'rocket age' when scientists were keen to explore the origins of life and the solar system. Carl Sagan died in 1996, by which time Brian was working on similar projects, continuing Sagan's work.

'I WENT TO THE LIBRARIAN AND ASKED FOR A BOOK ABOUT STARS... AND THE ANSWER WAS STUNNING. IT WAS THAT THE SUN WAS A STAR, BUT REALLY CLOSE. THE STARS WERE SUNS, BUT SO FAR AWAY THEY WERE JUST LITTLE POINTS OF LIGHT... THE SCALE OF THE UNIVERSE SUDDENLY OPENED UP TO ME.'

" I'm not absolutely sure of anything and there are many things I don't know anything about... I don't feel frightened about not knowing things, about being lost in the mysterious universe without having any purpose – which is the way it really is as far as I can tell. "

Richard Feynman

Another of Brian's science heroes is Richard Feynman – a theoretical physicist born in America in 1918. 'Many people have probably never heard of him,' Brian tells us, 'but to physicists, Richard Feynman was something of a legend.' Richard Feynman was involved in the development of the atom bomb during the Second World War. He was awarded Nobel Prize for physics in 1965. Brian has remarked on Richard Feynman's great ability to help the public understand more about science. Richard Feynman died in 1988.

" Richard Feynman is one of the most important and influential scientists of the 20th century, arguably as influential as Einstein. "

ARE YOU BEST MATES WITH...

Brian

By now you should know lots of things about Brian. Test your knowledge of him by answering these questions:

1 What did Brian watch on television at the age of one?

a) Scooby Doo
b) The first moon landing
c) Blue Peter

2 Where did Brian live as a boy?

a) The Moon
b) London
c) Chadderton

3 What was the name of the band that Brian first joined?

a) Take That
b) One Direction
c) Dare

4 What grade did Brian get in his maths A level?

a) D
b) A*
c) C

5 How tall is Brian?

a) 1.6 metres
b) 2.2 metres
c) 1.78 metres

6 What is Brian's middle name?

a) Edward
b) Einstein
c) Newton

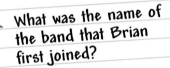

7 In which profession did Brian's parents work?

    a) Medical
    b) Banking
    c) Teaching

8 Which TV show does Brian co-host with Dara Ó Briain?

    a) Stargazing Live
    b) Wonders of Life
    c) Horizon

9 Which popular television drama did Brian give a lecture about?

    a) Coronation Street
    b) The X-Factor
    c) Doctor Who

10 Which instrument did Brian play in the band D:Ream?

    a) The triangle
    b) Keyboards
    c) Bass guitar

Answers

1 **b)** The moon landings
2 **c)** Chadderton
3 **c)** Dare
4 **a)** D
5 **c)** 1.78 metres
6 **a)** Edward
7 **b)** Banking
8 **a)** Stargazing Live
9 **c)** Doctor Who
10 **b)** Keyboards

You can find out more about Brian Cox by:

logging onto http://www.apolloschildren.com/brian

or http://www.manchester.ac.uk/research/brian.cox

or following him on Twitter @ProfBrianCox

Brian has written the following books:

Wonders of the Solar System, co-written with Andrew Cohen, published 2010 by Collins

Wonders of the Universe, co-written with Andrew Cohen, published 2011 by Collins

Wonders of Life, co-written with Andrew Cohen, published 2013 by Collins

Why Does E=mc2? (and why should we care?), co-written with Jeff Forshaw, published 2009 by Da Capo Press

The Quantum Universe: Everything that Can Happen Does Happen, co-written with Jeff Forshaw, published 2011 by Allen Lane

Quote sources

Page 4 The Daily Mail, 2012, Carpool on YouTube, 2010, The Telegraph, 2008; **Page 7** The Guardian, 2010; **Page 8** The Daily Mail, 2012; **Page 9** The Daily Mail, 2012; **Page 11** The Guardian, 2011, The Guardian, 2008; **Page 13** London Evening Standard, 2013, BBC Radio 4, 2008; **Page 15** Wonders of the Universe, 2011; **Page 17** TED.com, 2011; **Page 22** The Telegraph, 2011; **Page 23** The Telegraph, 2011, Carpool on YouTube, 2010; **Page 24** The Telegraph, 2011; **Page 25** BBC Radio 4, 2011, The New York Times, 1999.

Glossary

Apollo 11
The spaceflight that first landed human beings on the moon

Astronomer
A scientist who studies the universe

Atom bomb
A bomb that explodes from nuclear energy

Big Bang
A theory of how the universe began

Cosmos
The universe seen as a whole, ordered system

Documentary
A factual report using the evidence of real events

Ecosystem
A community of living things with non-living things

Einstein
A famous theoretical physicist

Honorary doctorate
A degree awared to people as an acknowledgement of their work

Inspiral Carpets
An indie rock band from Manchester

Jodrell Bank Observatory
A space observatory in Cheshire

Particle physics
A branch of physics which studies the nature of particles

PhD
Short for Doctor of Philosophy, a high-level academic degree

Physics
The part of science that looks at nature, matter and energy

Prestigious
Highly respected and important

Rational
Logical and well-reasoned

Syncopated
An unexpected rhythm, sometimes on the off-beat

Synthesized music
Electronically produced music

Terrorist
A person who uses terror tactics to make a political point

Top of the Pops
A TV show featuring chart music

INDEX